Animals at Risk

Contents

What puts animals at risk? 2
What puts pandas at risk? 4
Where can pandas live safely? 7
What puts sea turtles at risk? 8
Will pandas and sea turtles survive? 12
Risks for pandas and sea turtles 14

Written by Deborah Kespert

Collins

What puts animals at risk?

Some animals are at risk on land and at sea.

panda

sea turtle

They are at risk from people and animals. Their habitats can be harmed.

Not all animals can be kept safe in their own habitats.

Some need help from people or must live in animal reserves.

What puts pandas at risk?

Pandas live in thick bamboo forests far away from people. These forests are high in the mountains.

panda habitats

People cut down the soft bamboo shoots that pandas eat. They use the forest land for farming. This destroys the panda's habitat and food.

Some people hunt pandas. They sell their skins to make coats. Their fur is sold to make rugs.

Where can pandas live safely?

Many pandas now live in safe reserves in the mountains. Hunters cannot track them here and there is plenty of bamboo to eat.

What puts sea turtles at risk?

Sea turtles lay their eggs in nests on the sand at night. But some people steal turtle eggs for food.

turtle eggs

Animals eat turtle eggs too. Some turtles hatch and reach the sea safely, but they are still at risk.

Hermit crabs eat turtle eggs.

When sea turtles get bigger, people hunt them for their meat and paint their hard shells to sell.

When people go fishing, the turtles can get stuck on their fishing hooks or trapped in nets for catching fish.

Sea turtles are at risk on land and at sea.

Will pandas and sea turtles survive?

We need to take care of pandas and sea turtles to help them live longer.

More mountain reserves are needed to keep pandas safe.

Helpers collect turtle eggs from the beach and take them away to hatch safely.

All animals at risk need our care.

Risks for pandas and sea turtles

Pandas' food is destroyed.

People hunt pandas.

14

Animals eat sea turtle eggs.

People hunt sea turtles.

Turtles can get trapped in nets.

Ideas for reading

Written by Clare Dowdall, PhD
Lecturer and Primary Literacy Consultant

Learning objectives: *(reading objectives correspond with Blue band; all other objectives correspond with White band)* apply phonic knowledge and skills as the prime approach to reading unfamiliar words that are not completely decodable; read more challenging texts which can be decoded using their acquired phonic knowledge and skills, along with automatic recognition of high frequency words; draw together ideas and information from across a whole text; give some reasons why things happen

Curriculum links: Science, Citizenship

Focus phonemes: ur, i-e (survive), oy (destroys)

Fast words: the, to, we, what, puts, some, they, people, their, here, there, when, are, all, go, be, where, many, more, down

Resources: whiteboard, internet, pencils and paper

Word count: 291

Build a context for reading

- Show children the word *survive* written on a whiteboard. Focus on the digraph *ur* and practise sounding it out. Ask them to use their phonic knowledge to blend all the phonemes in the word.

- Discuss what the word *survive* means and ask children to put it into a sentence, e.g. *It is hard to survive without food.* Explain that this book is about animals that struggle to survive.

- Look at the front cover together and ask children to read the title and blurb. Ask children to suggest what the panda and turtle are at risk from. Check that children understand the term "at risk".

- Turn to the contents. Ask children to read through it to see how the information book is organised. Note how there is an introduction and then a chapter for each animal. Note how questions are used to organise the information.

Understand and apply reading strategies

- Turn to pp2–3. Model reading the text to the group, using phonic knowledge to decode unfamiliar words e.g. habitat, harmed, reserves.

- Discuss the content of these pages. Check that children are reading for meaning by asking simple questions, e.g. *What are animals at risk from? What is a habitat?*